SCOTTISH SONGS

SCOTTISH SONGS

Edited by Chris Findlater

Lomond

Compiled by RLS Ltd
© 1998 Waverley Books Ltd,
David Dale House,
New Lanark, ML11 9DJ

Lyrics to 'Scotland the Brave' © Cliff Hanley

ISBN 0 947782 33 8

Printed and bound by Mackays of Chatham

2 4 6 8 10 9 7 5 3 1

Contents

Annie Laurie — 8

Auld Lang Syne — 10

The Barnyards o' Delgaty — 12

The Blue Bell of Scotland — 14

Blue Bonnets Over the Border — 16

Bonnie Dundee — 18

Bonnie Wee Thing — 20

Ca' the Yowes to the Knowes — 22

Caller Herrin' — 24

The Campbells are Comin' — 26

Charlie Is My Darling — 28

Come O'er the Stream, Charlie — 30

Comin' Thro' the Rye — 32

Corn Rigs — 34

An Eriskay Love Lilt — 36

Fair Helen of Kirkconnell — 38

Farewell to Fiunary — 40

The Flowers o' the Forest — 42

Flow Gently, Sweet Afton — 44

The Four Maries — 46

Green Grow the Rashes, O — 48

A Hieland Lad — 50

Ho-ro, My Nut-Brown Maiden — 52

Contents

I Lo'e Na a Laddie But Ane	54
Jock o' Hazeldean	56
A Lewis Bridal Song	58
Loch Lomond	60
Macpherson's Rant	62
Mary of Argyle	64
My Ain Kind Dearie	66
My Love Is Like a Red, Red Rose	68
My Love, She's But a Lassie Yet	70
O May, Thy Morn Was Ne'er Sae Sweet	72
The Piper o' Dundee	74
The Rowan Tree	76
Scotland the Brave	78
The Skye Boat Song	80
Sugar Candy	82
The Uist Tramping Song	84
Wae's Me for Prince Charlie	86
The Wee Cooper o' Fife	88
When the Kye Come Hame	90
Wi' a Hundred Pipers	92
Ye Banks and Braes o' Bonnie Doon	94
Glossary	96

SCOTTISH
SONGS

Annie Laurie

Her brow is like the snaw-drift,
Her neck is like the swan;
Her face it is the fairest
That e'er the sun shone on.
That e'er the sun shone on,
And dark-blue is her e'e;
And for bonnie Annie Laurie
I'd lay me doun and dee.

Like dew on the gowan lying
Is the fa' o' her fairy feet;
And like winds in summer sighing,
Her voice is low and sweet.
Her voice is low and sweet,
And she's a' the world to me;
And for bonnie Annie Laurie
I'd lay me doun and dee.

William Douglas

Auld Lang Syne

We twa ha'e run aboot the braes,
And pu'd the gowans fine,
But we've wandered mony a weary foot
Sin' auld lang syne.

For auld lang syne, my dear,
For auld lang syne;
We'll tak a cup o' kindness yet,
For auld lang syne.

We twa ha'e paidl't in the burn
Frae morning sun till dine;
But seas between us braid ha'e roared
Sin' auld lang syne.

For auld, etc.

And surely I'll be your pint-stoup,
And surely you'll be mine;
And we'll tak' a cup o' kindness yet,
For auld lang syne.

For auld, etc.

And here's a hand, my trusty fere,
And gie's a haud o' thine;
And we'll tak' a richt gude willie-waucht
For auld lang syne.

For auld, etc.

Robert Burns

The Barnyards o' Delgaty

In New Deer par-ish I was born, A child of youth to Meth-lick came; And gin' ye'll no be-lieve my word the sess-ion clerk will tell the same.

Chorus

Lin-ten ad-ie, toor-in ad-ie, Lin-ten ad-ie, toor-in ae; Lin-ten, lour-in, lin-ten, lour-in, Lin-ten lour-in, lour-in lee.

As I cam' in by Netherdale,
At Turra market for to fee,
I fell in wi' a farmer chiel
Fae the barnyards o' Delgaty.

Linten addie, toorin addie,
Linten addie, toorin ae;
Linten, lourin, linten, lourin,
Linten, lourin, lourin, lee.

He promised me the ae best pair
That e'er I set my een upon:
When I gaed hame tae Barnyards
There was naethin there but skin and bone.

Linten addie, etc.

The auld black horse sat on his rump;
The auld grey mear lay on her wime:
For a' that I could hup and crack
They wouldna rise at yokin' time.

Linten addie, etc.

I can drink and nae be drunk;
I can fecht and nae be slain;
I can kiss another's lass,
And aye be welcome tae my ain.

Linten addie, etc.

My can'le noo it is brunt oot:
The snotter's fairly on the wane;
Sae fare ye weel, ye barnyards -
Ye'll never catch me here again.

Linten addie, etc.

The Blue Bell of Scotland

Oh where, and oh where, is your— High-land lad-die gone? Oh where, and oh where, is your— High-land lad-die gone? He's gone to fight the foe for King— George up-on the throne, And it's oh! in my heart I— wish him safe at home.

Oh where, and oh where, did your Highland laddie dwell?
Oh where, and oh where, did your Highland laddie dwell?
He dwelt in merry Scotland, where grows the sweet blue bell,
And it's oh! in my heart I love the laddie well.

Oh what, and oh what, does your Highland laddie wear?
Oh what, and oh what, does your Highland laddie wear?
He wears the plaided tartan around his form so fair;
And it's oh! in my heart I wish that he were here.

Blue Bonnets Over the Border

Chorus

March! March! Et- trick and Te- vi- ot- dale! Why, my lads, din- na ye march

G C G C D C G

for- ward in or - der? March! March! Esk- dale and Lid- des- dale, All the Blue Bon- nets are

C G D7 G G C G D7 G C Emin7

Verse

o - ver the bor - der! Ma - ny a ban - ner spread, Flut- ters a- bove your head,

G G C D7 G

Ma - ny a crest that is fa - mous in sto - ry! Mount and make rea- dy then,

G C G Emin D/F# G

sons of the moun- tain glen, Fight for your King, and the old Scot- tish glo - ry.

Emin Amin C G G/B G

March! March! Ettrick and Teviotdale!
Why, my lads, dinna ye march forward in order?
March! March! Eskdale and Liddesdale,
All the Blue Bonnets are over the Border!

Many a banner spread flutters above your head,
Many a crest that is famous in story!
Mount and make ready then, sons of the mountain glen,
Fight for your king, and the old Scottish glory.

Come from the hills where the hirsels are grazing,
Come from the glen of the buck and the roe;
Come to the crag where the beacon is blazing;
Come with the buckler, the lance and the bow.

Trumpets are sounding, war steeds are bounding,
Stand to your arms and march in good order.
England shall many a day talk of the bloody fray
When the Blue Bonnets came over the Border!

Bonnie Dundee

To the Lords of Con-ven-tion 'twas Clav'r-house who spoke: "Ere the King's crown shall fall there are crowns to be broke, Then each cav-a-lier who loves hon-our and me, Let him fol-low the bon-net of Bon-nie Dun-dee." Come fill up my cup,— come fill up my can, Come sad-dle your hor-ses, and call out your men, Un-hook the West Port— and let us gae free, And it's

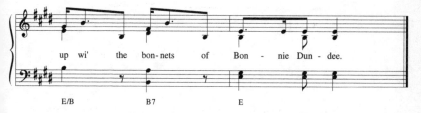

up wi' the bon-nets of Bon - nie Dun - dee.

E/B   B7   E

Dundee he is mounted, he rides up the street,
The bells are rung backward, the drums they are beat;
But the Provost, douce man, says "Just e'en let him be:
The toun is weel rid o' that de'il Dundee."

Come fill up my cup, come fill up my can,
Come saddle your horses, and call out your men,
Unhook the West Port, and let us gae free,
And it's up wi' the bonnets o' Bonnie Dundee.

"There are hills beyond Pentland, and lands beyond Forth;
Be there lords in the lowlands, they've chiefs in the north;
And brave dunie-wassals, three thousand times three,
Will cry Ho! for the bonnets of Bonnie Dundee.

Come fill up etc.

"Then away to the hills, to the caves, to the rocks:
Ere I own a usurper I'll couch with the fox;
And tremble, false Whigs, in the midst of your glee:
You have not seen the last of my bonnets and me."

Come fill up, etc.

Sir Walter Scott

Bonnie Wee Thing

Bon - nie— wee— thing, can - ty— wee thing, Love - ly— wee— thing,

G   C   G   C   D   C   Amin   Emin   C

wert thou— mine;   I— would   wear— thee   in— my— bo´ - som,

G   D7   G   G   C   G   C   D

Lest— my— jew - el   I   should— tine.   Wist - ful - ly— I—

C   D   G   G

look— and— lan - guish,   In that bon - nie   face of— thine;—   And my heart— it

C   G   G   Emin   D   C   G/D   D7   G

stounds   with   an - guish,   Lest— my— wee— thing   be   na— mine.

G   Amin   D7   C   Cmin   D   G

Bonnie wee thing, canty wee thing,
Lovely wee thing, wert thou mine;
I would wear thee in my bosom,
Lest my jewel I should tine.

Wit and grace and love and beauty
In ae constellation shine!
To adore thee is my duty,
Goddess o' this soul o' mine.

Robert Burns

Ca' the Yowes to the Knowes

Ca' the yowes to the knowes, Ca' them whar the hea - ther grows,

Ca' them whar the burn - ie rowes, My bon - nie dear - ie. As

I gaed down the wa - ter side, There I met my shep - herd lad, He

row'd me sweet - ly in his plaid, And ca'd me his dear - ie.

'Will ye gang down the water-side,
And see the waves sae sweetly glide
Beneath the hazels spreading wide,
The moon it shines fu' clearly?'

Ca' the yowes to the knowes,
Ca' them them whar the heather grows,
Ca' them whar the burnie rows,
My bonnie dearie!

'I was bred up in nae sic school,
My shepherd lad, to play the fool,
An' a' the day to sit in dool,
An' naebody to see me.'

Ca' the yowes, etc.

'Ye sall get gowns and ribbons meet,
Cauf-leather shoon upon your feet,
And in my arms ye'se lie and sleep,
An' ye sall be my dearie.'

Ca' the yowes, etc.

'If ye'll but stand to what you've said,
I'se gang with you, my shepherd lad,
And ye may row me in your plaid,
And I sall be your dearie.'

Ca' the yowes, etc.

'While waters wimple to the sea,
While day blinks in the lift sae hie,
Till clae-cauld death sall blin' my e'e,
Ye sall be my dearie.'

Robert Burns

Caller Herrin'

Wha'll buy cal - ler her - rin'? They're bon - nie fish and hale - some fa - rin':

G   D   G   Emin   A   D   D7

Verse

Buy my cal - ler her - rin', New drawn— frae the Forth! When

G   D   Emin   G   D7   G

ye were sleep - in' on your pil - lows, Dreamed ye aught o' our puir fel - lows,

D   G   D   G

Dark - ling as they face the bil - lows, A' to fill our wo - ven wil - lows?

D   G   C   A   D

Chorus

Buy my cal - ler her - rin', They're bon - nie fish and hale - some fa - rin';

G   D   G   Emin   A   D

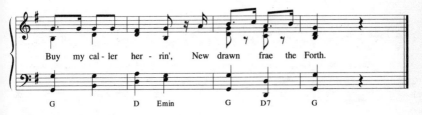

Buy my cal - ler her - rin', New drawn frae the Forth.

And when the creel o' herrin' passes,
Ladies, clad in silks and laces
Gather in their braw pelisses,
Toss their heads and screw their faces.
Buy my caller herrin'
New drawn frae the Forth.

Buy my caller herrin'?
They're bonnie fish and halesome fairin:
Buy my caller herrin',
New drawn frae the Forth!

Gude caller herrin's no got lightlie,
Ye can trip the spring fu' tightlie,
Spite o' tauntin', flauntin', flingin',
Gow has set you a' a-singin.
Buy my caller herrin'
New drawn frae the Forth.

Buy my etc.

But neebour wives, now tent my tellin',
When the bonny fish ye're sellin':
At ae word be aye your dealin' -
Truth will stan' when a'thing's failin'.
Buy my caller herrin'
New drawn frae the Forth.

Buy my etc.

Lady Nairne

The Campbells are Comin'

The Camp-bells are com-in', o-ho, o-ho! The Camp-bells are com-in', o-ho, o-ho! The Camp-bells are com-in', to bon-nie Loch Le-ven, The Camp-bells are com-in', o-ho, o-ho! U-pon the Lo-monds I lay, I lay— U-pon the Lo-monds I lay, I lay, I look-ed down to bon-nie Loch Le-ven, And saw— three bon-nie perch-es play.

The great Argyle he goes before,
He makes the cannons and guns to roar,
Wi' sound o' trumpet, pipe and drum,
The Campbells are coming, oho, oho!

The Campbells are comin', oho, oho!
The Campbells are comin' oho, oho!
The Campbells are comin', to bonnie Loch Leven,
The Campbells are comin', oho, oho!

The Campbells they are a' in arms,
Their loyal faith and trust to show,
Wi' banners rattlin' in the wind
The Campbells are coming, oho, oho!

The Campbells are coming, etc.

Charlie Is My Darling

Oh! Char-lie is my dar-ling, My dar-ling, my dar-ling, Oh! Char-lie is my dar-ling, The

Dmin   Gmin   Dmin   Dmin   Gmin

young Che-va-lier. 'Twas on a Mon-day morn - ing, Right ear-ly in the year, That

Dmin   A7   Dmin   A7   Dmin   A   Dmin

Char-lie came to our town, The young Che-va-lier. Oh! Char-lie is my dar-ling, My

B♭   F   Gmin Dmin   A   Dmin

(except last time)

1-5

dar-ling, my dar-ling, Oh! Char-lie is my dar-ling, The young Che-va-lier.

Gmin   Dmin   Dmin   Gmin   Dmin   A7   Dmin

As he cam' marching up the street,
The pipes play'd loud and clear,
And a' the folk cam' runnin' out
To see the Chevalier.

Oh! Charlie is my darling,
My darling, my darling,
Oh! Charlie is my darling,
The young Chevalier.

Wi' hieland bonnets on their heads
And claymores bright and clear,
They've cam' to fight for Scotland's right
And the young Chevalier.

Oh! Charlie, etc.

They've left their bonnie hieland hills,
Their wives and bairnies dear,
To draw the sword for Scotland's lord:
The young Chevalier.

Oh! Charlie etc.

Oh, there were mony beating hearts
And mony hopes and fears;
And mony were the pray'rs put up
For the young Chevalier.

Oh! Charlie etc.

Lady Nairne

Come O'er the Stream, Charlie

Come o'er the stream, Char - lie, dear Char - lie, brave Char - lie, Come

o'er the stream, Char - lie, and dine wi' Mac - Lean; And though you be

wea - ry we'll make your heart cheer - y, And wel - come our Char - lie, and

his loy - al train. We'll bring down the track dear we'll bring down the

black steer, The lamb from the breck - en and doe from the

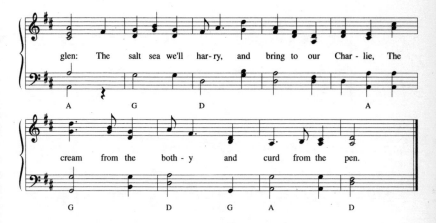

glen: The salt sea we'll har-ry, and bring to our Char-lie, The

A   G   D   A

cream from the both-y and curd from the pen.

G   D   G   A   D

And you shall drink freely the dews of Glen Sheerly
That stream in the starlight when kings dinna ken;
And deep be your meed of the wine that is red,
To drink to your sire and his friend the MacLean.

If aught will invite you, or more will delight you,
'Tis ready a troop of our bold Hieland men
Shall range on the heather with bonnet and feather,
Strong arms and broad claymores, three hundred and ten.

Come o'er the stream Charlie, dear Charlie, brave Charlie,
Come o'er the stream, Charlie, and dine wi' MacLean;
And though ye be weary we'll make your heart cheery,
And welcome our Charlie, and his loyal train.

Comin' Thro' the Rye

Gin a bo-dy meet a bo-dy, Com-in' thro' the rye;

Gin a bo-dy kiss a bo-dy, Need a bo-dy cry?

Chorus

Il - ka las-sie has her lad-die, Nane, they say, ha'e— I; Yet

a' the lads they smile at me, When com-in' thro' the rye.

Gin a body meet a body
Comin' frae the toon;
Gin a body greet a body,
Need a body froon?

Ilka lassie has her laddie,
Nane, they say, ha'e I;
Yet a' the lads they smile at me,
When comin' thro' the rye.

Amang the train there is a swain
I dearly lo'e mysel';
But what's his name; and what's his hame,
I dinna care to tell.

Ilka lassie has her laddie,
Nane, they say, ha'e I;
Yet a' the lads they smile at me,
When comin' thro' the rye.

Corn Rigs

It was u-pon a— Lam - mas night, When corn— rigs are bon-nie, O, Be - neath the moon's un - cloud - ed light, I held— a-wa' to— An-nie,— O; The time flew by— wi'— tent - less heed, Till 'tween the— late and ear-ly,— O, Wi' sma' per-sua - sion she a - greed— To see me— thro' the bar - ley,— O. Corn— rigs, and bar - ley rigs, Corn— rigs are

bon - nie___ O; I'll ne'er for - get that hap - py___ night,___ A -

D   E   A   D   E

mang the___ rigs wi'___ An - nie,___ O.

D   E   A

The sky was blue, the wind was still,
The moon was shining clearly, O;
I set her down wi' right good-will
Amang the rigs o' barley, O.
I kent her heart was a' my ain;
I loved her maist sincerely, O;
I kissed her ower and ower again,
Amang the rigs o' barley, O.

Corn rigs and barley rigs,
Corn rigs are bonnie, O;
I'll ne'er forget that happy night
Amang the rigs wi' Annie, O.

I locked her in my fond embrace,
Her heart was beating rarely, O;
My blessings on that happy place,
Amang the rigs o' barley, O.
But by the moon and stars so bright,
That shone that hour so clearly, O;
She aye shall bless that happy night
Amang the rigs o' barley, O.

Corn rigs, etc.

I ha'e been blithe wi' comrades dear,
I ha'e been merry drinkin', O;
I ha'e been joyful gatherin' gear;
I ha'e been happy thinkin', O.
But a' the pleasures e'er I saw,
Though three times fairly doubled, O:
That happy night was worth them a',
Amang the rigs o' barley, O.

Corn rigs, etc.

Robert Burns

An Eriskay Love Lilt

Vair me o— ro van o, Vair me o— ro van ee, Vair me o, ru o ho, Sad am I with-out thee. When I'm lone-ly dear white heart, Black the night or wild the sea; By love's light my foot finds The old path - way to thee.

Last time only Verse

Vair me o, o rovan o,
Vair me o, o rovan ee,
Vair me o, ru o ho,
Sad am I, without thee.

When I'm lonely, dear white heart,
Black the night or wild the sea;
By love's light my foot finds
The old pathway to thee.

Vair me o, etc.

Thou'rt the music of my heart,
Harp of joy, o cruit mo chridh;
Moon of guidance by night,
Strength and light thou'rt to me.

Vair me o, etc.

Fair Helen of Kirkconnell

I wish I were where Hel - en lies, For night and day on___ me she cries; For night and day on___ me she cries, I wish I were where Hel - en lies On___ fair Kirk-con - nell___ lea.___ Oh Hel - en fair! Oh Hel - en chaste! Were I with thee I___ would be blest, Were I with thee I___ would be blest, Where thou liest low and at thy rest On___ fair Kirk - con - nell___ lea.___

Oh Helen fair, beyond compare
I'll make a garland of thy hair;
I'll make a garland of thy hair,
Shall bind my heart for evermair
Until the day I dee.
Curst be the heart that hatch'd the thought,
And curst the hand that fired the shot;
And curst the hand that fired the shot,
When in my arms burd Helen dropt,
And died to succour me.

O think na but my heart was sair,
My love dropt down and spak nae mair;
My love dropt down and spak nae mair,
O think na ye my heart was air
On fair Kirkconnell lea.
I found my foe behind a wa';
I lighted doun my sword to draw,
I hacked him in pieces sma,
I hacked him in pieces sma,
Who took my love from me.

I wish I were where Helen lies,
For night and day on me she cries;
I wish I were where Helen lies
On fair Kirkconnell lea.

Farewell to Fiunary

The wind is fair, the day is fine, And swift-ly, swift-ly runs the time; The

G　D　Amin　D　Emin　C　D

boat is float-ing on the tide, That wafts me off from Fiu-na-ry.

Emin　C　Amin　Bmin　C　Bmin　D7　G

Chorus

We must up and haste a-way, We must up and haste a-way,

G　Amin　D　Emin　Amin　Emin　D

We must up and haste a-way, Fare-well, fare-well to

Amin　C　Amin　G　C　Bmin

1.2. Fiu-na-ry.　3. Fiu-na-ry.

D7　G　D7　G

A thousand, thousand tender ties
Awake this day my plaintive sighs;
My heart within me almost dies,
At thought of leaving Fiunary.

We must up and haste away,
We must up and haste away,
We must up and haste away,
Farewell, farewell to Fiunary.

But I must leave these happy vales,
See, they spread the flapping sails!
Adieu, adieu my native dales,
Farewell, farewell, to Fiunary.

We must up etc.

Norman MacLeod

The Flowers o' the Forest

I've seen the smi - ling of For - tune be - guil - ing, I've

tast - ed her fa - vours and felt her de - cay:

Sweet was her bless - ing and kind her ca - ress - ing, But

now they are fled, fled far a - way.

I've seen the for - est a - dorn'd the fore - most Wi'

I've seen the morning wi' gold the hills adorning,
And loud tempests roaring before parting day;
I've seen Tweed's silver streams, glitt'ring in the sunny beams,
Grow drumlie and dark as they roll'd on their way.

O fickle fortune, why this cruel sporting?
Why so perplex us poor sons of a day?
The frown cannot fear me; thy smile cannot cheer me,
Since the Flowers o' the Forest are a' wede away.

Flow Gently, Sweet Afton

Thou stockdove whose echo resounds thro' the glen,
Ye wild whistling blackbirds in yon thorny den;
Thou green-crested lapwing, thy screaming forbear –
I charge you, disturb not my slumbering fair.

How pleasant thy banks, thy green valleys below,
Where wild in the woodlands the primroses blow;
There oft as mild ev'ning sweeps over the lea,
The sweet-scented birk shades my Mary and me.

Thy crystal stream, Afton, how lovely it glides
And winds by the cot where my Mary resides;
How wanton thy waters her snowy feet lave,
As gath'ring sweet flow'rets she stems thy clear wave.

Flow gently, sweet Afton, among thy green braes,
Flow gently, sweet river, the theme of my lays;
My Mary's asleep by thy murmuring stream,
Flow gently, sweet Afton, disturb not her dream.

Robert Burns

The Four Maries

I ha'e but just begun to live,
And yet this day I dee;
Oh, tie a napkin ower my face,
That the gallows I mayna see.

My father kissed me and little thought,
When last he looked on me,
That I his last and lo'eliest wean
Should hang on a gallows tree.

Oh little did my mother ken,
The day she gi'ed me breath,
That I should come sae far frae hame
And die a shameful death.

For if my father and mother got wit,
And my bold brethren three,
Oh, mickle wad be the guid red blood
That day wad be spilt for me.

Green Grow the Rashes, O!

There's nought but care on ev-'ry han', In ev-'ry hour that pass-es, O; What sig-ni-fies the life o' man, An' 'twere na for the lass-es, O.

Chorus

Green grow the rash-es, O! Green grow the rash-es, O! The sweet-est hours that e'er I spend, Are spent a-mang the lass-es, O!

The warldly race may riches chase,
An' riches still may fly them, O;
And though at last they catch them fast,
Their hearts can ne'er enjoy them, O.

Green grow the rashes, O!
Green grow the rashes, O!
The sweetest hours that e'er I spend,
Are spent amang the lasses, O!

Gi'e me a canny hour at e'en,
My arms about my dearie, O;
An' warldly cares, and warldly men
May a' gae tapsalteerie, O.

Green grow etc.

For you sae douce, wha sneer at this,
Ye're nought but senseless asses, O;
The wisest man the warld e'er saw,
He dearly loved the lasses, O.

Green grow etc.

Auld Nature swears, the lovely dears
Her noblest work she classes, O;
Her prentice han' she tried on man,
And then she made the lasses, O.

Green grow etc.

Robert Burns

A Hieland Lad

A— Hie-land lad my— love was born, The Law-land laws he

held in scorn; But he still was faith—fu'— to his clan, My— gal-lant braw— John—

Chorus

Hie-land man. Sing— hey! my braw John Hie-land man! Sing

ho! my braw John— Hie-land man! There's— no' a lad— in—

a' the lan' Was— match— for— my— John— Hie-land-man!

Wi' his philabeg and his tartan plaid,
And gude claymore down by his side;
The ladies' hearts he did trepan –
My gallant braw John Hielandman!

Sing hey! my braw John Hielandman,
Sing ho! my braw John Hielandman,
There's no a lad in a' the lan'
Was match for my John Hielandman.

They banish'd him beyond the sea,
But ere the bud was on the tree,
Adown my cheek the pearlies ran,
Embracing my John Hielandman.

Sing hey! etc.

But oh, they caught him at the last,
And bound him in a dungeon fast;
My curse upon them every wan –
They've hanged my braw John Hielandman!

Sing hey! etc.

Ho-ro, My Nut-Brown Maiden

Ho - ro my nut - brown maid - en, Hi - ri my nut - brown maid - en, Ho -
ro - ro, maid - en! Oh she's the maid for me.

Her eye so mild - ly beam - ing, Her look so frank and free, In
wak - ing and in dream - ing, Is ev - er - more with me.

O Mary, mild-eyed Mary,
By land, or on the sea,
Though time and tide may vary,
My heart beats true to thee.

Ho-ro my nut-brown maiden,
Hi-ri my nut brown maiden,
Ho-ro-ro, maiden!
Oh, she's the maid for me.

In Glasgow or Dunedin
Were maidens fair to see;
But ne'er a Lowland maiden
Could lure mine eyes from thee;

Ho-ro, etc.

Mine eyes that never vary
From looking to the glen,
Where dwells my Highland Mary
Like wild-rose 'neath the Ben.

Ho-ro, etc.

And when with blossom laden,
Bright summer comes again,
I'll fetch my nut-brown maiden
Down frae the bonnie glen.

Ho-ro, etc.

I Lo'e Na a Laddie but Ane

I— lo'e na a lad-die but ane,_____ He lo'es na a las-sie but me;— He's wil-lin' to make me his ain,_____ And his ain I am wil-lin' to be._____ He coft me a rok-ley o' blue_____ And a pair_____ o' mit-tens sae green;_____ He vow'd that he'd ev-er be true,_____ And I plight-ed my troth_____ yes-treen._____

Let ithers brag weel o' their gear,
Their land and their lordly degree,
I care na for aught but my dear,
For he's ilka thing lordly to me.
His words mair than sugar are sweet,
His sense drives ilk fear far awa';
I listen, poor fool, and I greet –
But how sweet are the tears as they fa'!

"Dear lassie," he cries wi' a jeer,
"Ne'er heed what the auld anes will say;
Though we've little to brag of, ne'er fear,
What's gowd to a heart that is wae?
Our laird has both honours and wealth,
Yet see how he's dwinin' wi' care;
Now we, though we've naething but health,
Are canty and leal ever mair."

"O Menie, the heart that is true
Has something mair precious than gear;
Ilk night it has naething to rue;
Ilk morn it has naething to fear.
Ye warldlings gae hoard up your store,
And tremble for fear lest ye tine;
Guard your treasure wi' lock, bar and door –
True love is the guardian o' mine."

Jock o' Hazeldean

"Why weep ye by the tide, la-dye, Why weep ye by the tide?___ I'll wed ye to my young-est son, And ye shall be his bride; And ye shall be his bride, la-dye, Sae come-ly to___ be seen:" But aye she loot the tears down fa, For Jock o' Ha - zel - dean.

"Now let this wilful grief be done,
And dry that cheek so pale:
Young Frank is chief of Errington,
And lord of Langley-dale.
His step is first in peacefu' ha',
His sword in battle keen."
But aye she loot the tear doon fa'
For Jock o' Hazeldean.

"A chain of gowd ye shall not lack,
Nor braid to bind your hair;
Nor mettled hound, nor managed hawk,
Nor palfrey fresh and fair.
And you the foremost o' them a'
Shall ride our forest queen."
But aye she loot the tear doon fa'
Foe Jock o' Hazeldean.

The kirk was deck'd at morning-tide,
The tapers glimmer'd fair;
The priest and bridegroom wait the bride,
But ne'er a bride was there.
They sought her baith by bower and ha':
The ladye wasna seen;
She's ower the Border and awa'
Wi' Jock o' Hazeldean.

A Lewis Bridal Song

I'd sail with you to Mia-vaig in Uig, E'en tho' in twi-light, e'en tho' in twi-light.

G   D   G D   G   Amin   C   Emin   C

I'd sail with you to Mia-vaig in Uig, E'en thro' the dark and the sea - mist.

G   D   Emin   G   D   G

How shall we fare when the wind's in the sail, and storm clouds ga - ther,

C   Emin   Bmin

storm clouds ga - ther? How shall we fare in the whirl of the gale

Emin   C   Emin

Out in the midst of the Is - lands? Mo - rag bheag of the gold - en hair,
Who is the maid - en who dances with joy, Like

D   Emin   Emin   C   G

Fine

Fair as the dawn - ing, fair as the dawn - ing, Mo - rag bheag of the
foam on the wave - tops, foam on the wave - tops? Who is the maid on the

Bmin   B7   Emin   C   G

gold - en hair, Light - ly she stepped to her bri - dal.
danc - ing floor? She is the bride who came sail - ing.

C   G   Bmin   D   C

D.C.

Loch Lomond

By yon bon-nie banks and by yon bon-nie braes, Where the

sun shines bright on Loch Lo - mond, Where me and my true love were

e - ver wont to gae, On the bon-nie, bon-nie banks o' Loch Lo - mond. O,

ye'll tak' the high road, an' I'll tak' the low road, An' I'll be in Scot-land a -

fore ye; But me and my true love will ne - ver meet a - gain On the

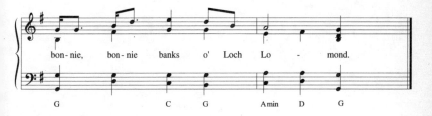

bon - nie,   bon - nie   banks   o'   Loch   Lo - mond.

G   C   G   Amin   D   G

'Twas there that we parted in yon shady glen,
On the steep, steep side o' Ben Lomond
Where in purple hue, the Hieland hills we viewed;
And the moon comin' out in the gloamin'.

O, ye'll tak' the high road, an' I'll tak' the low road,
An' I'll be in Scotland afore ye;
But me and my true love will never meet again
On the bonnie, bonnie banks o' Loch Lomond.

The wee birdies sing, and the wild flowers spring,
While in sunshine the waters are sleeping;
But the broken heart kens nae second spring again,
Though the waefu' may cease frae their greetin'.

O, ye'll tak' the high road, etc.

Lady John Douglas Scott

Macpherson's Rant

Fare - weel ye dun - geons dark and strong, Fare - weel, fare - weel to

thee. Mac - pher - son's time will no be— long On

yon - der gal - lows tree. Sae ran - tin'- ly, sae wan - ton - ly, Sae

daun - tin'- ly gaed he, He played a tune and he

daunced it roun' A - bou' the gal - lows tree.

Chorus

(Last time)

'Twas by a woman's treacherous hand
That I was condemn'd to dee.
Above my head at a window she stood
And a blanket threw ower me.

Sae rantin'ly, sae wantonly,
Sae dauntin'ly gaed he,
He played a tune, and he danced it roun'
About the gallows tree.

Untie these bands fae aff my hands
And gi'e tae me my sword;
And there's nae a man in all Scotlan',
But I'll brave him at a word.

Sae rantin'ly etc.

There's some come here for tae see me hang,
And some tae buy my fiddle;
But ere I come tae pairt wi' her,
I'll brak her doon the middle.

Sae rantin'ly etc.

He took his fiddle in baith his hands
And brak it ower his knee;
And said, when I am deid and gone
Nae ither shall play thee.

Sae rantin'ly, etc.

The courier came ower the brig o' Banff
Tae set Macpherson free –
But they put the clock a quarter afore,
And hanged him fae the tree.

Sae rantin'ly, etc.

Mary of Argyle

I have heard the ma-vis sing-ing His love song to the morn; I have

G   C   G   Amin   D   G

seen the dew-drop cling-ing To the rose just new-ly born; But a

C   G   D7   G

sweet-er song has cheer'd me, At the ev'-ning's gen-tle close; And I've

Emin   B7   Bmin   Emin

seen an eye still bright-er Than the dew-drop on the rose. 'Twas thy

A7   D   A7   D

voice my gen-tle Ma-ry, And thine art-less win-ning smile, That

G   C   G   Amin   D   G

made this world an E - den Bon - ny Ma - ry of— Ar- gyle.

Tho' thy voice may lose its sweetness,
And thine eye its brightness too;
Tho' thy step may lack its fleetness,
And thy hair its sunny hue;
Still to me wilt thou be dearer
Than all the world shall own –
I have loved thee for thy beauty,
But not for that alone.
I have watch'd thy heart, dear Mary,
And its goodness was the wile
That has made thee mine for ever,
Bonny Mary of Argyle.

My Ain Kind Dearie

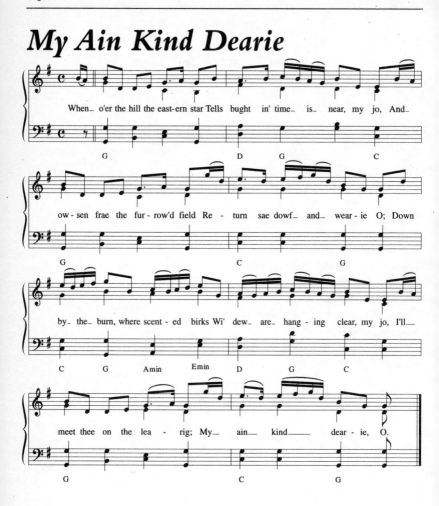

When o'er the hill the east-ern star Tells bught in' time is near, my jo, And

ow-sen frae the fur-row'd field Re-turn sae dowf and wear-ie O; Down

by the burn, where scent-ed birks Wi' dew are hang-ing clear, my jo, I'll

meet thee on the lea-rig; My ain kind dear-ie, O.

In mirkest glen at midnight hour
I'd rove and ne'er be eerie, O,
If thro' that glen I gae'd to thee,
My ain kind dearie, O.
Altho' the nicht were ne'er sae wild,
And I were ne'er sae weary, O,
I'd meet thee on the lea-rig,
My ain kind dearie, O.

The hunter lo'es the morning sun,
To rouse the mountain deer, my jo;
At noon the fisher seeks the glen,
Along the burn to steer, my jo;
Gi'e me the hour o' gloamin' grey,
It maks my heart sae cheerie, O,
To meet thee on the lea-rig,
My ain kind dearie, O.

My Love Is Like a Red, Red Rose

Oh my love is like a red, red rose, That's new - ly sprung in June; Oh my— love is like the mel - o - dy That's sweet - ly played in tune. As fair thou art, my bon - nie lass, So deep in love am I; And— I will love thee still, my dear, Till a' the seas gang dry; Till— a' the seas gang dry, my dear, Till a' the seas gang dry; And—

Till a' the seas gang dry, my dear,
And the rocks melt wi' the sun;
And I will love thee still, my dear,
While the sands o' life shall run.

While the sands o' life shall run, my dear,
While the sands o' life shall run;
And I will love thee still, my dear,
While the sands o' life shall run.

And fare thee weel, my only love,
O fare thee weel a while;
And I will come again, my love,
Tho' 'twere ten thousand mile.

Tho' 'twere ten thousand mile, my love,
Tho' 'twere ten thousand mile;
And I will come again, my love,
Tho' 'twere ten thousand mile.

Robert Burns

My Love, She's But a Lassie Yet

My love she's but a lass - ie yet, My love she's but a

A

lass - ie yet, We'll let her stand a year or twa, She'll

E   A   D   A

no be half sae sau - cy yet. I rue the day I

D   E   A   E7

socht her, O I rue the day I socht her, O Wha

A   D   E

gets her need - na say she's woo'd, But he may say he's bocht her, O!

A   E   A   E   A   D   E   A

Come draw a drap o' the best o't yet,
Come draw a drap o' the best o't yet;
Gae seek for pleasure where ye will,
But here I never missed it yet,

We're a' a dry wi' drinkin' o't,
We're a' a dry wi' drinkin' o't;
The minister kissed the fiddler's wife
And couldna preach for thinkin' o't.

Robert Burns

O May, Thy Morn Was Ne'er Sae Sweet

O May, thy morn was ne'er sae sweet as the mirk night o' December! For spark-ling was the ro-sy wine, And pri-vate was the cham-ber: And dear was she I dare-na name, But I will ay re-mem-ber: And dear was she I dare-na name: But I will ay re-mem-ber.

And here's tae them that, like oursel
Can push about the jorum;
And here's tae them that wish us weel –
May a' that's guid watch o'er them.
And here's tae them we daurna tell –
The dearest o' the quorum!

Robert Burns

The Piper o' Dundee

He play'd "The Welcome owre the Main",
And "Ye'se be Fou' and I'se be Fain",
And "Auld Stuart's Back Again",
wi' muckle mirth and glee.
He play'd "The Kirk", he play'd "The Quier",
The "Mullin Dhu" and "Chevalier",
And "Lang Awa', but Welcome Here",
Sae sweet, sae bonnilie.

And wasna he a roguie, a roguie, a roguie?
And wasna he a roguie,
The piper o' Dundee?

It's some gat swords, and some gat nane,
And some were dancing mad their lane;
And mony a vow o' weir was ta'en
That night at Amulree.
There was Tullibardine, and Burleigh,
And Struan, Keith and Ogilvie;
And brave Carnegie, wha but he,
The piper o' Dundee!

And wasna he etc.

The Rowan Tree

Oh!— Row-an Tree, Oh! Row-an Tree! thou'lt aye be dear to me,— En-twin'd thou art wi' mo-ny ties, o' hame and in-fan-cy. Thy leaves were aye the first o' spring, Thy flow'rs the sim-mer's pride; There was nae sic a bon-ny tree in a' the coun-trie-side. Oh!— Row-an Tree.

How fair wert thou in simmer time, wi' a' thy clusters white,
How rich and gay thy autumn dress, wi' berries red and bright.
On thy fair stem were many names, which now nae mair I see,
But they're engraven on my heart; forgot they ne'er can be.
Oh! Rowan Tree.

We sat aneath thy spreading shade, the bairnies round thee ran;
They pu'd thy bonny berries red, and necklaces they strang.
My mother! Oh, I see her yet, she smiled oor sports to see,
Wi' little Jeanie on her lap, and Jamie at her knee.
Oh! Rowan Tree.

Oh, there arose my father's prayer, in holy evening's calm;
How sweet was then my mother's voice, in the Martyr's psalm.
Now a' are gane. We meet nae mair, aneath the Rowan tree;
But hallowed thoughts around thee twine, o' hame and infancy.
Oh! Rowan Tree.

Scotland the Brave

Hark when the night is fall-ing, Hear! hear the pipes are call-ing,

D

Loud - ly and proud-ly call-ing, down thro' the glen.

G   D   E7   Asus4   A

There where the hills are sleep-ing, Now feel the blood a-leap-ing,

D

High as the spi-rits of the old High-land men.

G   D   G   D

Chorus

Tower - ing in gal-lant fame, Scot - land my moun-tain hame,

A   A7   D   G   D

78

High in the misty Highlands,
Out by the purple islands,
Brave are the hearts that beat beneath Scottish skies;
Wild are the winds that greet you,
Staunch are the friends that meet you,
Kind as the light that shines from fair maidens' eyes.

Towering in gallant fame,
Scotland, my mountain hame,
High may your proud standards gloriously wave.
Land of my high endeavour,
Land of the shining river,
Land of my heart forever,
Scotland the brave.

Cliff Hanley

The Skye Boat Song

Speed, bon-nie boat, like a bird on the wing, On-ward, the sai-lors cry;___ Car-ry the lad that's born to be king O - ver the sea to Skye.___ Loud the winds howl, loud the waves roar, Thun-der-claps rend the air;___ Baf - fled, our foes stand by the shore; Fol - low, they will not dare.___

Speed bonnie boat, like a bird on the wing,
Onward, the sailor's cry;
Carry the lad that's born to be king,
Over the sea to Skye.

Though the waves leap, soft shall ye sleep;
Ocean's a royal bed.
Rocked on the deep, Flora will keep
Watch by your weary head.

Speed bonnie boat, etc.

Many's the lad fought on that day,
Well the claymore could wield:
When the night came, silently lay
Dead on Culloden field.

Speed bonnie boat, etc.

Burned are our homes, exile and death
Scatter the loyal men;
Yet ere the sword cool in the sheath,
Charlie will come again.

Speed bonnie boat, etc.

Harold Boulton

Sugar Candy

There was a wee lassie awfy thin, A bundle o' bones wrapped up in skin, Now she's gettin' a wee double chin, Wi' eatin' sugar candy.

Chorus

Ally bally, ally bally bee, sittin' on your mammy's knee, Greetin' for another bawbee To buy some sugar candy.

Puir wee Johnnie's greetin' too:
What can his puir mammy do,
But gi'e them a penny atween them two,
To buy some sugar candy.

Ally bally, ally bally bee,
Sittin' on your mammy's knee,
Greetin' for another bawbee,
To buy some sugar candy.

Here's a penny, ma bonnie wee man,
Rin doon the road as fast as ye can,
Dinna stop till Coulter's van,
An' buy some sugar candy.

Ally bally, etc.

The Uist Tramping Song

Chorus

Come a - long, come a - long, Let us foot it out to - ge - ther; Come a -

long, come a - long, Be it fair or storm - y wea - ther, With the

hills of home be - fore us And the pur - ple of the hea - ther, Let us

sing in hap - py cho - rus, Come a - long, come a - long. So—

Verse

gai - ly sings the lark, And the sky's all a - wake With the

pro - mise of the day, For the road we glad - ly take; So it's
heel and toe and for - ward, Bid - ding fare - well to the town,—— For the
wel - come that a - waits us Ere the sun goes down.

Come along, come along,
Let us foot it out together;
Come along, come along,
Be it fair or stormy weather,
With the hills of home before us
And the purple of the heather,
Let us sing in happy chorus,
Come along, come along.

It's the call of sea and shore,
It's the tang of bog and peat,
And the scent of brier and myrtle
That puts magic in our feet;
So it's on we go, rejoicing,
Over bracken, over style;
And it's soon we will be tramping
Out the last, long mile.

Come along, etc.

Hugh Roberton,
from the Gaelic of
Archibald MacDonald

Wae's Me for Prince Charlie

A wee_ bird_ cam' to our ha'_ door, He war - bled_ sweet_ and_ clear - ly, And aye_ the_ o'er come o'_ his_ sang, Was "Wae's me_ for Prince Char - lie." Oh! when_ I_ heard the bon - nie, bon - nie bird, The tears_ came_ drap - pin' rare - ly: I took_ my_ bon - net aff_ my_ head For weel_ I_ lo'ed Prince Char - lie.

Quo' I, "My bird, my bonnie, bonnie bird,
Is that a tale ye borrow?
Or is't some words ye've learned by rote
Frae a lilt o' dule and sorrow?"
"Oh, no, no, no," the wee bird sang,
"I've flown sin' morning early,
On sic a day o' wind and rain –
Oh, wae's me for Prince Charlie!

"On hills that are by rights his ain
He roves, a lonely stranger;
On ilka hand he's pressed by want;
On ilka side by danger.
Yestreen I saw him in a glen;
My heart near bursted fairly,
For sairly changed by want was he –
Oh, wae's me for Prince Charlie!

"Dark night cam' on, and tempest howl'd
Loud ower the muirs and valleys;
And where was it your Prince lay down,
Wha's hame should been a palace?
He row'd him in a Hieland plaid
That cover'd him but sparely,
And slept beneath a bush o' broom –
"Oh, wae's me for Prince Charlie!"

But now the bird saw some red-coats,
And shook his wings wi' anger.
Cried he, "This land is no for me:
I'll tarry here nae langer."
A while he hovered, on the wing,
Ere he departed fairly,
But aye the o'ercome o' his sang
Was "Wae's me for Prince Charlie!"

The Wee Cooper o' Fife

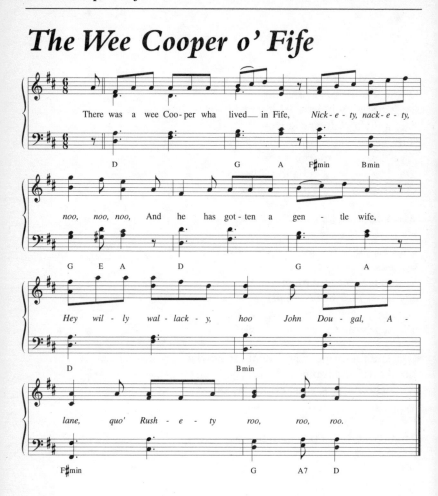

She wadna bake, and she wadna brew,
Nickety, nackety, noo noo noo,
For spoilin' o' her comely hue;
Hey willy wallacky, hoo John Dougal,
Alane, quo' Rushety, roo roo roo.

She wadna card, and she wadna spin,
Nickety, nackety, etc.
For thinkin' o' her gentle kin;
Hey willy wallacky, etc.

The cooper has gone to his wool-pack,
Nickety, nackety, etc.
And laid a sheep-skin on his wife's back;
Hey willy wallacky, etc.

I'll no thrash ye, for your gentle kin,
Nickety nackety, etc.
But I will thrash my ain sheep-skin.
Hey willy wallacky, etc.

Oh, I will bake and I will brew,
Nickety, nackety, etc.
And think nae mair on my comely hue;
Hey, willy wallacky, etc.

Oh, I will card, and I will spin,
Nickety, nackety, etc.
And think nae mair on my gentle kin;
Hey willy wallacky, etc.

All ye wha hae gotten a gentle wife,
Nickety, nackety, etc.
Just think ye on the wee cooper o' Fife,
Hey, willy wallacky, etc.

When the Kye Come Hame

'Tis not beneath the burgonet
Nor yet beneath the crown,
'Tis not on couch of velvet
Nor yet on bed of down;
'Tis beneath the spreading birch
In the dell without a name,
Wi' a bonnie, bonnie lassie
When the kye come hame.

Awa' wi' fame and fortune:
What comforts can they gi'e?
And a' the arts that prey upon
Man's life and liberty!
Gi'e me the highest joy
That the heart o' man can frame:
My bonnie, bonnie lassie
When the kye come hame.

James Hogg

Wi' a Hundred Pipers

Chorus

Wi' a hun - dred pi - pers an' a', an' a', Wi' a hun - dred pi - pers an'

a', an' a', We'll up an' gie them a blaw, a blaw, Wi' a hun - dred pipers an'

a', an' a'. O', it's owre the Bor - der, a - wa', a - wa', It's

owre the Bor - der, a - wa', a - wa', We'll on an' we'll march to

Car - lisie ha', Wi' its yetts, its cas - tle, an' a', an' a'. Wi' a

hun - dred pi - pers an' a', an' a', wi' a hun - dred pi - pers an'

D   G   D   E7

a', an' a', We'll up an' gie them a blaw, a blaw, Wi' a

A   D   G

hun - dred pi - pers an' a', an' a'.

D   A   D

Oh, our sodger lads look'd braw, look'd braw,
Wi' their tartan kilts, and a' and a'
Wi' bonnets, feathers and glitterin' gear,
An' pibrochs soundin' sweet and clear.
Will they a' return to their ain dear glen?
Will they a' return, oor Hieland men?
Second-sichted Sandy look'd fu' wae,
And mithers grat as they marched away.

Wi' a hundred pipers an' a', an' a',
Wi' a hundred pipers an' a', an' a',
We'll up an' gie them a blaw, a blaw,
Wi' a hundred pipers an' a', an' a'.

Oh, wha is foremost of a', of a'?
Oh, wha does follow the blaw, the blaw?
Bonnie Charlie, the Prince o' us a', hurrah!
Wi' his hundred pipers, and a', and a'.
His bonnet and feathers he's wavin' high,
His prancin' steed just seems to fly,
The nor' wind sweeps thro' his golden hair,
An' the pibrochs blaw wi' an unco flare.

Wi' a hundred pipers etc.

Lady Nairne

93

Ye Banks and Braes o' Bonnie Doon

Ye banks and braes o' bonnie Doon, How can ye bloom sae fresh and fair? How can ye chant ye little birds, And I sae weary fu' o' care? Ye'll break my heart, ye warbling bird That warbles on the flow'ry thorn, Ye mind me o' departed joys, Departed never to return.

Oft ha'e I roved by bonnie Doon
To see the rose and woodbine twine;
And ilka bird sang o' its love,
And fondly sae did I o' mine.
Wi' lightsome heart I pu'd a rose,
Fu' sweet upon its thorny tree:
But my fause lover stole my rose,
But Ah! he left the thorn wi' me.

Robert Burns

Glossary

a': all
aught: anything.
auld lang syne: days of long ago.
bawbee: small coin, halfpenny.
bheag: little (Gaelic)
bogle: apparition.
braid: broad
braw: fine.
brunt: burnt.
burd: lady, damsel.
burgonet: knightly helmet.
caller: fresh
canty: happy
chiel: chap.
creel: fish basket.
cruit mo chridh: dear harp of
   mine (Gaelic).
dule: sad fate.
douce: quiet, sedate.
Dunedin: Edinburgh.
dunie-wassal: follower of a
   Highland chief.
eerie: afraid.
fecht: fight.
fee: to be hired.
fere: companion.
froon: frown.
gae: go.
gang: go
gear: goods
ghaist: ghost.
gloamin': twilight.

Gow: Niel Gow, the violinist,
   composer of the original tune.
gowan: daisy.
gowd: gold.
greet: weep.
hairst: harvest.
hirsel: flock.
ilk, ilka: each, every.
jeer: brag, proclaim.
jorum: bottle, punch-bowl.
kent: knew.
kye: cows.
leal: true,
leglin: milk-pail.
lyart: grey.
mickle, muckle: much.
mear: mare.
Menie: form of Marian.
pair: pair of horses.
pearlies: tears.
philabeg: kilt.
pibroch: pipe music.
tapsalteerie: topsy-turvy.
tent: pay attention.
tine: lose
Turra: Turriff.
unco: remarkable
wae: woe.
wean: child.
willie-waucht: powerful swig.
wime: belly.